RECKON

RE CK ON

Steve
McOrmond

Brick Books

Library and Archives Canada Cataloguing in Publication

McOrmond, Steve, 1971–, author
    Reckon / Steve McOrmond.

Poems.
Issued in print and electronic formats.
ISBN 978-1-77131-482-4 (softcover).—ISBN 978-1-77131-484-8(PDF).
—ISBN 978-1-77131-483-1 (EPUB)

    I. Title.

PS8575.O74R43 2018   C811'.54   C2017-907251-X
                                   C2017-907252-8

We acknowledge the Government of Canada, the Canada Council for the Arts, and the Ontario Arts Council for their support of our publishing program.

The author photo was taken by Semco Salehi.
The book is set in Dante.

Cover image:
Plate XXI of "Studies among the Snow Crystals . . ." by Wilson Bentley.
From Annual Summary of the "Monthly Weather Review" for 1902.
Image ID: wea02089, NOAA's National Weather Service (NWS) Collection
Location: Vermont, Jericho
Photo Date: 1902 Winter

Design and layout by Marijke Friesen.
Printed and bound by Sunville Printco Inc.

Brick Books
431 Boler Road, Box 20081
London, Ontario N6K 4G6

www.brickbooks.ca

For Janet

Far factories are busy making apples
made of plastics, all of them equally real.

—*Graham Foust, "The Old Thing"*

CONTENTS

Bodilies

Pastoral

This morning, I heard a blue jay belting out scurrilous antilyrics from its perch in the backyard cherry tree. My first thought was of a *Songbird Symphony* CD I own and how great it sounds through headphones.

And last night, by the light of the clichéd moon, a pair of skunks turned sod for the writhing underneath.

And the refrigerator on autodefrost, chirping like crickets in a field.

And we mask our bodilies with the lavender notes of a Glade plug-in.

And doctors have removed a gallbladder from a patient 6,000 miles away by remote control.

And mouse brains were the first to be grown.

And almost a hundred horses died during the making of *Ben-Hur*.

And the Jarvis Model JR-50 Robotic Hog Head Dropper can process 1,200 pigs an hour.

And I cannot claim that no animals were harmed in the making of this poem.

And the good poison can only be found in Chinatown.

And who is sufficient for these things?

For your kid's next birthday party, why not make it special with a one-hour, in-home reptile show featuring snakes, lizards, and turtles? Add a real gator for only $49.99.

The newlyweds, unlocking the door of their first apartment in the city and snapping on the light, were not alone. The kitchen floor and countertops quivered and convulsed with cockroaches. Rapid eye movement. There and gone.

And an age ago, after a pleasant day at the beach, when the boy's mother pulled his T-shirt over his head, it was full of hornets.

And nature, a green door. Locked from the inside. Trespassers will be violated.

And we felt fortunate to live in the afterglow of Steve Jobs, although we worried about trans fats for a while.

When I surprised the raccoon lurking in the alcove outside my front door, it bared its teeth before humping, Quasimodo-like, across the busy road. The approaching headlights confused it and, though I ran to the curb and waved my arms, the taxi didn't slow or even try to miss it.

In the video game, I'm running through the jungle with a knife in my hand, prepared to do harm. There's a glitch in the frame rate. The foliage jitters; lush ferns disintegrate into jagged frozen pixels, unsuspending disbelief.

And the tree of heaven has a runny root, says the gardener on the radio call-in show. Cut it down, it'll come up where you least expect.

And what do they open, the keys that come rotoring down from the maple trees?

And there's no denying the beauty. *Photo Spot Presented by Coca-Cola.*

And the parkway is congested, as always.

And off in the distance, I can't tell where the sky ends and the lake begins.

And the buildings downtown decapitated by fog.

And the air smells like burning tires, and I love it here, I really do.

We: Current Exhibition

Our momentum seemed unstoppable,
right up until we were siphoning
gas from abandoned cars. The primitive
animation like a cave painting
set in motion: Wile E. Coyote, in headlong
pursuit of his prize, sprints over
the canyon rim, hind legs pinwheeling
in an immense Technicolor
emptiness. It isn't until he thinks
to look down that he becomes
a sack of stones.

The Upstarts

No longer content with a minimal life treading water
in heated pools, they organize like stevedores.
It takes heavy lifting, coercion, and cajoling to jury-rig
molecules into membranes, hermitic cells into makeshift
communities. Next on the to-do list: learn to breathe
topside and get the knack for locomotion. Their flight
from hydrosphere to lithosphere, from single-celled
self-sufficiency to social networking takes, oh, a billion years.
Then one day the littoral zone up and lurches onto land.
Headstrong and vulnerable, accident- and error-prone,
their bodies mostly water, they venture forth, over the dunes
and across the plains. Eventually, their upwardly mobile
offspring populate the earth from sea to sea, a prodigal sprawl,
giving rise to aqueducts, theism, pi, even the likes of you and me.

Cats and Dogs

Rain, rain, rain on the roof
like a noise machine—you've been listening
but you can't hear the loop.
You aren't alone. The past holds itself aloof
like a cat, absolutely certain
it's the most captivating and misunderstood
creature in the room. Present
company included. The future is the twin
that couldn't be more different.
Anxious as a dog leashed to a lamppost,
it knows its master, who's just run in
for cigarettes, might not be coming back,
that things are always in the process
of never being the same again. This,
like a bowl on the verge of empty, warrants
hypervigilance. The past drapes itself
around your neck, a suffocating,
purring pelt. Of course it's self-satisfied.
It's made it this far. The future twitches and jerks
in its sleep, chasing some small frantic
thing that leaves the perfume of its panic
on the air. No one tells you how
hard it will be to ignore them, pawing
at the door to be let out, in, out, in, out again.

Eviction Notice

They're neat party tricks, I'll give you that.
When I wasn't looking, you swapped my hands
for papier-mâché copies of your own.
How do you do it? Making me believe
I can hear you using the table saw in the basement
workshop when I live on the eleventh floor?
A voice, a tendril of aftershave, cigarette
smoke (your brand) wafting down the hall.
I'm jerked awake, afraid something's on fire.
When I fly into a rage, dinner-table talk
devolving into a blood sport, it's your barbs
my dummy mouth spits out. My wife holds
her ground; the cat pancakes from the room.
It's time you quit the premises. We can't go on
living like china in a bull shop. It's not
as though I'm putting you out on the street.
You have the spacious heavens to roam,
a million-acre farm. You mean to say
there's no place you can grow your roses?
I never could talk to you; now it's even worse.
Pregnant ellipses . . . non sequiturs. I should
try a Ouija board. How can I grieve properly
when you just won't leave? You always did
show up unannounced, staying as long
as you damn well pleased. I never stood
up to you when you were alive, but now
you must vacate and surrender the property.
I asked you nicely. I'm not asking anymore.

Rilke for Voice and Guitar

Your better angels are AWOL.
The loyal ones you could do without:
the angel of the enlarged prostate,
the angel of arrhythmia, her hummingbird wings.

You just pray you don't lose your mind,
rolling brownouts in the neocortex, verbal
incontinence, saying the damnedest things:
where's the baby and *who stole my cheese?*

Overheard at the ultrasound lab:
"The neck came in early; the neck's done.
The thyroid's in the waiting room.
The bladder isn't here yet."

A friend has a stash of pills
she calls her golden parachute,
worries she won't have the nerve
or be able to keep them down.

You've searched high and low
for one of those Cold War false molars
with the cyanide capsule still intact,
but they don't appear on eBay.

Everyone has an exit strategy,
though we seldom put them to use.
Another carrot is dangled
and we keep stumbling along.

This morning, you went for a walk,
accompanied, as usual, by the angel
of arthritis; every step a little jolt of pain,
tacks casually tapped into knee joints.

The young woman jogged past you
so quickly she created her own cool
breeze. Were you ever so lively
and at ease in your body? For the moment,

you were in the slipstream of her scent:
good clean sweat, sweet and tart.
Fruit and seaweed? Lemon grass and cedar?
It's been awhile since you nosed a glass.

Her ponytail swayed from side to side,
her calves rippled. She swooshed through the air.
A pinch of that buoyancy—she'd never miss it—
and you'd dance with the nurses till lights out.

Big Gulp

Has anyone in recorded history
actually cried over spilt milk?
By the hot foods case in which
wieners and taquitos rotate in perpetuity,
the sumptuous glister of grease under glass,
I fumbled the just-filled cistern,
watched it topple in slo-mo,
the fountain Coke gushing out,
a tsunami over the tiles. I'll confess
I nearly wept. The cashier's mild contempt
as he called for an unseen subordinate
to bring the mop and pail. Who cares
if it causes cavities, unclogs drains,
strips the rust off an old pocket knife
I found buried in the garden? Is it apocryphal
that the cops carry two gallons
in the trunks of their cruisers to scour
blood from the road after an accident?
I don't feel like googling it right now.
This I know for certain: all forms
of happiness are a calculated risk.
We should treasure it up—life's
concentrated sweetness, its carnal
stickiness and fizz, the shock of it
on the tongue—while we can.
Why order off the menu when
there's an all-day buffet? Oh,
to be as animated as bubbles, as frivolous
as liquid sugar. *Slurp-slurp! Glug-glug!* So what
if our appetites betray us, if our poking

straws are never satisfied, not even after
they've touched bottom and sucked it dry?
We are ugly but we have the Cheetos.

Self-Portrait as Archaic Torso

Oil on beaverboard

The bathroom mirror's bevelled edge lops off
the head, amputates both legs above the knee.
What's left of him crowds the frame within a frame.
Notice the fulsome chest, almost feminine, and how
the nipples, thick mahogany daubs, stare balefully;
the prodigious belly that everywhere precedes him,
his unofficial envoy in matters of home and state.
Such an unheroic posture you will not find
set in stone at the palace gate. Did he stoop
his whole life so as not to stand out in a crowd?
Observe how the fleshy abundance, skin a wintry
alabaster veined with blue, is bowed like a shelf of snow,
making the ordinary bits that dangle below appear
fragile and insignificant, hardly worth the bother
of defiling with mallet, chisel, crude plaster leaf.
The stonemason's apprentice can knock off early.
Not so fast: this minor monument has a bone
to pick with beauty. See how the canvas
has been overworked, the weave clogged
with layer upon layer of paint, as though
the artist couldn't decide which form to free?
He was never one thing, but the game is fixed.
You have to dance with the one that brought you.
In his youth, he was happy playing *show me yours*
with the boy next door and with the boy's
sisters too. It was all good. These days, he slings
his laptop bag onto a rolled-over shoulder,
goes to work and to the liquor store
every day or two as to a greengrocer.

Trim the fat, lose the flavour, his mother used to say.
Midafternoons are extra lean; the emaciated hands
on the office clock crawl toward quitting time
when he may retire from the graceless now,
remove his armour and revel in what
he's made of. A plenitude of cravings,
marbled perfection. He doesn't skimp.

Evolved from the Invisible

From "Studies among the Snow Crystals During the Winter of 1901–2, with Additional Data Collected During Previous Winters," by Mr. Wilson A. Bentley, dated Jericho, Vt., June 10, 1902

This branch of study is as yet
at its beginning; it still possesses
the charm of novelty; many of its problems
are unresolved. Doubtless the actual
connection between forms and sizes
and the temperature and density of the air
is much more intimate than our present
knowledge would indicate. Violent winds
cause fractures to occur, and whenever, as must
often happen, subsequent growth takes place
around and upon such broken crystals,
irregular, unsymmetrical forms result.
Considerable modifications are due
to the aggregation of amorphous or
granular material, the lines obliterated,
every angle so deeply coated over
and imbedded with it that the true
character does not reveal itself, except
under the closest examination. Frail,
light and branching forms are rendered
course and heavy by such additions,
so that they fall quickly to the earth.

Introduction to Unarmed Combat

From Unarmed Combat, *Edmond Cloutier,*
Printer to the King's Most Excellent Majesty, Ottawa, 1940

No two opponents will attack
in precisely the same way. Do not be misled
by false cries into relaxing a lock or hold.
Over the methods employed, there must be no
scruple or compunction. To gain the absolute
mastery over one's foe, kicking or gouging
of the eyes, though foreign and detestable,
must be used without hesitation. You will learn,
through constant practice with a variety of partners,
to acquit yourself in the most desperate
of situations. Against an armed combatant,
the unarmed man can and should
by a skillfully timed offensive action
secure the upper hand. A short section
dealing with the methods of carrying
a wounded man has been included.
There is a certain similarity of holds
although the object is quite different.

An Arkansas Love Story

The dismal he did so well,
it went down easy. Mama

always said he had a voice
for radio ministry. You got along

like a barn fire. You had whiled
away the humid afternoon together

under the shade tree with a pile of books,
a fresh pack of smokes and a bottle

you passed back and forth with ceremony.
The lawn needed mown; you drank

to the weeds. Gradually his eyes grew dark
and fiercely sad. You retired early, whereupon

with three quick taps on his breastbone,
he pursued the thought that had nagged him

all day long like a deer fly. Maybe our deaths
are trapped inside, desiring to be set free.

Like a possum caught in the crawl space
or a wasp between panes. You couldn't tell

if it was a question or something he knew
for certain. Upon his naked chest, you laid

both palms flat. Congenital defect, you said,
then pushed hard so that he staggered

back and sprawled, laughing, on the bed
atop your grandma's quilt, which was,

as it happened, just where you wanted him.

It Pains Me to Recall

The robin's egg I stole from the nest; it was so blue.
The fox skull high on the mantelpiece
I coveted so greatly I learned to climb,
and that I had a gift for falling.

My most earnest and considered desires
I spilled to a mall Santa with onions on his breath,
and snooping in my mother's bureau I found
my baby teeth in a costume jewellery box.

My father kissed me on the forehead,
said he'd be away a couple of days
on a business trip to Des Moines—
who gets gone in Des Moines?

It's a minor mystery devoid of grandeur,
like an amateur magician doing sleight of hand
at the county fair; the silver dollar vanishes,
reappears behind a gap-toothed boy's left ear.

Consigned for a time to three tiny rooms
above a thrift store, we found holes
in our sweaters and my mother said we'd
carry the moths with us wherever we went.

Rust in the water, old blood singing
under primer and paint, I'd lie awake
as the feathered boas downstairs came to life,
some slithering, others trying in vain to fly.

The Policyholder

Long after they've gone to bed—
the wife, the child who cries—
he sits up with a bottle of scotch,
reading the insurance company's
handbook. Every loss is assigned
an amount payable: a thumb
is worth three fingers, the vision
in one eye is equal to the hearing
in both ears. Half the principle sum.
It isn't solace he seeks, but plainness.
At the bookstore, he stood before a wall
of self-help guides, each glossy cover
promising the answer, and walked out
with the latest Ian Rankin—pretty tame
compared to the underwriters, the nameless
who catalogue the debasements
of flesh and spirit. Their talent for the telling
detail, gruesome and mundane, is hard
to beat—extremity pumps, colostomy supplies,
bloodletting devices. He could skim,
but reads every word. Penance and exegesis.
Not that there aren't moments of genuine
pathos: for failure of a reattached limb
and its removal within one year. Imagine
accepting that slim hope, only to have the body
reject it as false. The good-for-nothing
servant, having twice deserted its duties,
tossed out with the sharps and reams
of bloody gauze. His glass empties
and refills itself. He stays up because
sickness sours the sheets and the only thing

that works is bleach, so their bedroom reeks
like the oncology ward. He kisses her cheek
because he can taste it on her lips—
one of the routine slights for which
he must atone. For breast prostheses,
surgical brassieres, and certain drugs
listed in the compendium. For wigs.

I Want to Love More

To feel the horses in my chest as I did
when I was young and hell-for-leather
to land the first kiss. To make it look easy
like knobby-kneed old men playing tennis
in their immaculate white shorts;
they never seem to break a sweat.
To admit that at dawn the city is nearly adorable,
rubbing sleep from its eyes. The shoe repair guy
flips the sign in the window, lugs a five-foot-tall
red fibreglass cowboy boot to the curb.
The barista stifles a yawn. Above it all,
the crane operator has the best seat in the house.
To grasp before I go what any kindergarten
teacher knows: you can make anything
with glitter, hearts, and glue. But who am I
trying to fool? I'm no good at it: every ode
I attempt is simultaneously mistranslated
into elegy. No sooner do I resolve to call
and tell you the sunrise is, at this very moment,
painting the undersides of the clouds
pale yellow, salmon, and rose—look,
you can see the brushstrokes—than a car alarm
galls me from my reverie. My mixture
isn't right; I can never quite shake
the loneliness of living in this serene republic,
the longing that nests in the names
of racehorses: Waiting on a Woman, Dusty Lane
Galaxy, Escape the News, Nurse Thy Bitterness.
Oh, I do. Black coffee, dry toast on a chipped plate.

Birds Fall Dead

Birds Fall Dead in Arkansas

> "The first victims were the countless birds...."
> —*Ovid,* Metamorphoses

On her front porch in Heber Springs,
the country singer
shot the dog, then herself.

Exact same spot her man shot himself
a month before. On the front porch.
Ain't that a hell of a thing?

Makes me think of the blackbirds.

Which?

Them that fell / two years in a row.

Oh, I remember now.
The ones with the pretty
red shoulders.

✦

Blackbirds / starlings / cowbirds / grackles

collide in midair, bounce off car hoods,
pinwheel into shop windows, strike
lampposts, slap against vinyl siding,
get clotheslined by electric wires.
They nosedive into asphalt.

Ma'am, I was just wonderin'
why all these birds are, like,
falling from the sky?

Please hold.

✦

Eyewitnesses can't be trusted,
they always use words
like *eerily quiet*.

Stars fell on Alabama.
In Arkansas, dead birds.

Ma'am, it's just they're all over
the church steps.

Panic flight / nightmare fuel

✦

The explain-away

The secular apologetic

The suspicioned cover-up

The big conceal

✦

The college professor on TV:

It's a normal occurrence.
The sky is full of birds,
we're talking billions.

This time of year, they roost
in huge flocks. Imagine a thousand
birds in a single tree.

Any loud bang or flash
can incite a riot of wings.

These few that fell here, it's terrible,
but they don't amount to much.

✦

At the diner, in the supermarket
checkout line, and over the counter
at the Loans & Gun Shop, folks
have their own theories:

White trains

Cargill ammonia like a killing jar

Something to do with Pine Bluff

HAARP

Devil's music

Weird rain, surely
we did conspire it.

✦

The retired school bus driver:

Same time last year it was the drum fish.
The brown waters of the Arkansas
spit them up, a hundred thousand
dead and rotting all along
the riverbank from the Ozark Dam
to Hartman, must be twenty miles.

Well, I tell you what,
it didn't smell like Jesus.

Feller from Game and Fish
said it was disease, but I don't know.
Like the sign on the church lawn says,
Get an expert opinion! Ask God.

✦

Five thousand birds, the streets
slick with feathered gore.
One damned thing after another.

Ma'am, you still there?

Thanks for holding.
Someone from Animal Care and Control
will be along to clean them up.

The official cause of death:
blunt-force trauma.

✦

The court stenographer:

To tell the truth,
I was watching the Shopping Channel
when the birds started to fall.

Sparkles with the brilliance of hand-cut
faux gems and shimmering glitter.

The hand-painted figurine
fills the flat screen, shown
much larger than actual size.

✦

The concrete cutter (part-time):

Me and the girlfriend—
she's been living down in Lafayette—
we had some catching up to do.

We slept through it,
guess you could say.

Whole world could've
come crashing down, we
wouldn't have heard a thing.

✦

Nicotine-stained fingers / wine-dark aureole

Now, at home in your spare time,
without any previous schooling.

Come this way you lucky people.
The reckoning / happens every day.

✦

Your call is important to us.

Cell towers / wind turbines / tall buildings

They circle and circle
a fixed light

until they're too tired
to beat their wings
any longer.

If you are between 18 and 45 and in pain,
you may qualify for the clinical trial.

✦

That suicide in Cleburne county,
the one that followed the other,

should she have begrudged him
the everydayness

they never got to share?
Or counted herself spared?

✦

The people on the Internet:

How bad does a place have to get
for the birds to commit mass suicide?

Well, we are talking Arkansas—the state
that gave birth to Walmart and Bill Clinton....

The birds most likely drank
"fracking" waste water.

I remember massive undulating clouds
of blackbirds.... Now I only see "flocks"....

So last year the fish
got spooked and swam into each other?

On the morning of Dec 31, 2010, I woke up
and shared 2 dreams I had w/ 4 friends.
One of them was without question
the very story above. . . .

Albert [sic] Hitchcock?!?! O_o

✦

In America's most dangerous / little town,
the Delta bluesman hunkers down
in his wheelchair. Can't play
his polio butter-knife blues
since he had his stroke,
but his voice ain't broke.
He can still sing,
can really let it wail.

I say, if you like fat women,
come on down to Pine Bluff, Arkansas.

Done got trampled in a stampede
when someone pulled a gun,
but them blackbirds—
never seen the like.

You know, there's more fat women down there
than any place I ever saw.

34

The urinals are packed with ice.
There's pinkish puke on the floor—
in it, a boot skid.

Scrawled in Sharpie in the stall:
Whatever happens I will come.

    ✦

Birds in a single tree

Fish rotting on a stretch of riverbank

Parts per million of ammonia

Empty ton containers for stockpiling hazardous waste

Square feet of storage at Pine Bluff Arsenal

Canisters of white phosphorus

Drums that contained chemical matériel

Temperature and time required to decontaminate

    ✦

Guess I'll have to look it up.

Which?

The definition of normal.

✦

The lay minister swears
the birds started to plummet
at the stroke of midnight, as if
punctuality was a trademark
of the divine. The decorated
veteran of the war in Iraq, age 22,
lines his ball cap with aluminum foil—
but who'd want to read his mind?

If you've been hurt in a slip and fall,
contact one of our lawyers today.

The company I keep
when I keep seeing signs.
Shiver my patented genes.

(Another commercial break)

✦

She shot the damn dog.

Come again?

That country singer.
She had two little boys.
Bad enough they got to lose
their mother, but the dog?

Sometimes the fruit / rots before it ripens.
You know what I'm saying.

Mr. Alterations

We: Source Code

We were dropped out of nothing.
We fell and called it home.

The world that preceded us
was our white space. It had no immunity.

Our restlessness was a fever. This cave,
this valley—it was never enough.

We gnawed the bones, sucked
the marrow, then moved on.

We wandered far and wherever we went
we left rubbish tips and scars.

We learned to speak
and what we said was: *Get a load of us.*

We warred and suffered, traced
in soft clay images of the hunt.

We learned to carry fire
and then to make it. At first, it whispered:

Come closer, be warm, but it wasn't long
before we heard in its sibilance

a different proposition: *Burn
your neighbours, yes, burn everything.*

We were fast learners. We invented
writing so we could take down

what the fire said, account for our spoils
and keep track of what was owed: a goat,

a daughter, one's spear on short notice.
Once we had words, we sent them

on ahead of us to the four corners
and what we wrote was: *Yield*.

Uncanny Valley

Mornings, I like to be the first in. Swipe
my card, punch a PIN to disengage the alarm.

Then I can take my time. Sip chai,
have a scroll through the junk bin: *Hold*

Your Willy Super Stiff. Celebrities Use Açai Elite.
No emoji for how I'm feeling. Nothing is quote

unquote real anymore. My jeans are too tight.
I'm fastidious about clearing my history.

Deep in an offshore data centre, my vagaries
are tracked, time-stamped, mined

for meaningful adjacencies. Hard drives spin up,
ripping a near bit-perfect bootleg of my brain.

When I crush my deadlines, my boss says
I am a machine. He means it as praise,

and I accept it as such, with the requisite degree
of *aw shucks* and freshly whitened teeth.

A horripilation of dread cascades across my skin.
One of us doesn't quite register as human.

For the Beauty of Winona Ryder

Is that really you, Winona, wandering the aisles
of this 24-hour Duane Reade on West 58th below
Columbus Circle where Ferlinghetti watched
the retired ballerinas walking their dogs in the park
in the winter dusk. Gliding through the cough and cold
section, you look the part, your body fluid
in its movements, bird-boned, slight. Your days
as Hollywood's angsty ingenue behind you now,
no longer the *première sujet*. If it is you, Winona,
cleverly disguised as yourself, your secret is
safe with me. I won't ask for an autograph or selfie.
I think we're the same age. We've grown up together.
Now we're both "mid-career," which always makes me
picture a car careening off a cliff. The halfway point
of any long flight is the hardest. Winona, I know
you've had your ups and downs. The fans trigger-happy
in their adoration and reproach. I've seen the interviews.
Noni, Noni, Noni! Strangers screaming your name
behind the barricades: It's a certain kind of spooky,
but you can't complain. No one likes a malcontent.
When I fall, I pick myself up, keep walking
as though nothing happened. When you stumble,
news vans line the block. Tomorrow, early,
I'll claim my conference pass at the Javits Center—
I've colleagues who collect them, put them on display
in their offices, dangling from multicolored lanyards.
You study a package of lozenges, adjusting distance,
squinting to bring the ingredients into focus, but oh,
those eyes, those dark, glittering eyes—Joan of Arc.
Where will you go after this, will you drive around

all night in your Mercedes, listening to *Achtung Baby*?
Winona, we need you now more than ever,
this world is broken in ways we never bargained for.
Nobody asks *What's your damage?* anymore.

Introduction to Homelessness

> "The point is that fashion is the armour to survive
> the reality of everyday life."
>
> —*Bill Cunningham*

Old running shoes sans socks, a tattered cape
made of shopping bags skilfully knotted together
so they overlap like shingles on a roof or oily feathers,
your doom chic might make the cover of an un-
airbrushed, alt *Vogue*. Worn by a skin-and-bones
blonde on a runway in Milan, it'd be, like, *ooh la-effing-la*.
"Dashiell, it's not polite to point." A moment ago,
they were snapping selfies on the steps of the NYPL,
now the boy tugs at his father's coat sleeve, "Can I
have some money for that man over there?"
You're as much a fixture as those famous stone lions,
but no one wants their picture taken with you.
Dad shoots a glance your way, as if to say,
I think you can be safely ignored. But Dashiell
won't be deterred. With a slight, smug smile,
the man's face softens: he's taught his kid right.
He shrugs, fishes for his wallet, "Well, go on,
hurry up." The boy approaches shyly with his offering
only to have you—who knows why?—politely refuse it.
And now Dad is really annoyed; his son's return
is like the long walk back to the bench after striking out.
How dare you zombie-shuffle through
their father-son vignette, take the shine off
a perfectly good day? You merely smile and bow,
makeshift cloak crackling in the cold.

The Path of the Hero

To get to work, I have to walk
past the ghost bike. Lovingly
painted white, its panniers
planted with plastic flowers, petals
spattered with slush from passing cars,
this DIY memorial is a reprimand.
I try not to be distracted. I look both ways.

On the corner, there's Mr. Alterations.
The seamstress is already at her station
in the front window. I like to watch
her work. Surrounded by bobbins
and spools of coloured thread, how expertly
she feeds another pant leg to the machine.

Next door, there's the pet store
selling hungry cats and dogs. Just last week,
a young man with a binder and the most
earnest smile you ever saw stopped me
to discourse on the dark satanic
puppy mills churning out the cute.
I'd take all the darlings home
if I could. Which reminds me, I must
buy circus tights or a new blue suit
that means business. Maybe tomorrow.

Night of the Sitcoms

After another day
in which we do neither
harm nor good, this
is what it wants: for us to fall
asleep with our eyes open,
sweet dreams.
The bread is sprayed with
lacquer, there's no plumbing
under the sink, the stairs
dead-end in air. No one
lives here, no one
could. Crawling along
the bottom of the screen, a line
of severe storms.

We Like You for This

What is your name? What is your real name?
Have you voluntarily participated in a riot?
Have you crawled through the rubble
of Saturday night? Have you seen the light?
Were you expecting someone else? At this hour?
Have you ever picked food off the floor and eaten it?
When was your last confession? Do you mind if I smoke?
Does the run in my partner's stocking arouse you?
Do you want to be struck? Are you an actual person?
The evidence is circumstantial. We can neither confirm
nor deny. Do you know your family history? Are you prone
to mental infirmity? Have you ever been confined
in a prison or similar institution? Does God communicate
with you through visions? How's that
working out for you? Have you suffered? Would you say
you have a tendency to aestheticize suffering?
Do you get annoyed by the "fake" cheeriness of others?
Do these questions irritate you? Where were you standing
exactly when you say you saw the character assassin
turn the weapon on himself? Why should we believe
anything you say? Have you achieved? Are you paid
what you're worth? Does the mirror
regret to inform you? Have you felt the burn?
How many drinks do you have in a day? Are you sober now?
Do you commonly have a sour taste in your mouth?
Do you often have to apologize for your bad moods?
Is there always "something wrong" in your life?
Are you looking for that glorious appearing?
Who you gonna call? At this hour? Who is your disciple?
Write it down. When was the last time your heart
Evel-Knieveled over the abyss? Are you ready

to do the right thing? Have you claimed the greatness
of your soul's evolution from the locker at the bus station?
Did you think your birth a divine endorsement,
that you could go on living off the interest
like a trust fund baby?

Wilderness of Signs

Fire yoga, bubble tea, tank top for lady. Sorry
we're open. Keys cut here. Schnitzel Queen,
Shawarma's King, Ukrainian and Chinese
perogies. Specials all weak, come on in.

Depleted Uranium Jesus, organic vegan
spray tan, Borrowed Rice Tattoo. Siamese
side of building, this area not for walking
dogs. Wake up, Sheeps! Make sure empty
the pockets before put clothes in the machine.

Women! Get fit swinging from the pole.
Mattress warehouse sale, free spicy salmon roll.
Dolphins rape people, God loves Uganda.
Smile, you're on camera. Pain-free living,
for appointment call. Safety helmets must
be worn. Wash cut blow go. Pardon our dust.

The Signature

"I'm sorry, it doesn't match the one on file...."
You're just doing your job, Denise,

and you have a nice smile, but this notion of
making one's mark is pretty quaint. As proof

we are who we say we are, definitive it ain't.
We're just not ourselves today. In our defence,

the counter pen, globby ballpoint
on a short leash, cramped our flourish.

Anyway, the essential self is a fiction,
more like a nesting doll set, infinity edition.

You wouldn't know it, but it's awfully
crowded in here, so many left-

and right-handed versions, we can't keep
them all straight. There's no *I* in *teem*.

Why, we can't even agree on what not
to wear. You think this shirt was my idea?

We are the real deal, Denise, and this
inconvenience has us royally pissed, so if

you'll just cash our cheque, we can
all breathe a collective sigh of relief.

But it's clear from your demeanor
that you woke up feeling focused and singular,

and who are we—your finger a hair's breadth
from the silent alarm—to disabuse you?

Pure Outrage

Like Pluto, I have been demoted,
exiled to an out-of-sight, out-of-mind
cubicle beyond the Xerox. The light is bad,
the smell of toner sours the local air.
Central heating doesn't reach this far.
I get headaches. My left eye has developed
a twitch. I've refrained from quoting Marx
in the software user guide, endured
the office potlucks, and this is my reward?
In my performance review, it says
I lack engagement. It isn't true. Eccentric
though I may be, inclined to follow my own
wonky path round the sun, I'm linked in
at the cellular level, sensitive to perturbations
in the economy, passionate about living
the company's values every day. I'm so engaged,
it's pathetic, really. Walking to work
one cold morning not so long ago,
I arrived too late to witness the birth
of tragedy, though I almost stepped
in its gory aftermath: the jelly donut
leaking red onto the sidewalk, a crime scene.
I pictured a child of indeterminate age,
eyes all pupil, as the sticky confection—
at that moment, it stood for all the world
has to offer or withhold—slipped
from frozen fingers. I had meetings
and deadlines to keep, but I lingered,
I'll admit, with my head bowed low
because someone should be left to mourn.
Passersby didn't know what to make of it;

their postures stiffened, they steered wide.
What occurred to put me temporarily
out of service, I can't exactly tell.
Call it an isolated incident (it's happened
before), chalk it up to exhaustion (I sleep well).
If push came to shove, I'd guess it was
a near-life experience. No comment
field in the employee review form for that.

Atrium

Sunlight lampoons itself. The food court,
long disabused of its pretentions

to plein-airism, peddles burgers, biryani,
assembly-line sushi in shrink-wrapped trays,

the tables arrayed around a miniature Trevi
Fountain where the chronically wishful

cast loose change. Ersatz oasis
between East and West, the imaginatively

named office towers where we trade
time on an exchange that never rests.

Revolving doors, release us! We've heard
it's a lovely day out there to loaf

like those Pillsbury clouds. Pity the palm trees
for not being fake. Pity the common sparrow

jabbing at a French fry with its blunt beak;
the custodian, himself a refugee, who shakes

a dirty mop to frighten the bird off. It flits
as high as the vaulted glass will allow.

Temp

After you navigate the recorded voices,
I'm the real person who finally answers.
You're forgiven for not recognizing

the difference. Loosely affiliated
but basically unattached, it isn't true
that I get no benefits; today, I am entrusted

with an access card, a ring with many keys.
When the office printer stops working,
it's Someone Else's Problem: that

would be me. I pop the hatches, peer
into cramped compartments, as if
I know what the parts are supposed to do.

If there's a jam, it must be deep inside.
The printer resembles a heart, no,
strike that, the prototype

space capsule at the Smithsonian
designed to send a dog into orbit.
All progress demands sacrifice.

The fax machine didn't get the memo:
dusty and resolute in its twilight years,
it's still used by window cleaners to send flyers.

The mailroom is in the building's bowels,
labyrinthine corridors, dying fluorescents
that could trigger a seizure. I hate to go alone.

Invited by a colleague for drinks after work,
I can't think of an excuse. Can you believe
his business card, *Global Segment Manager,*

Non-Life? If you can, get this: I still go home
with him. My employers are like boyfriends.
They need me, just not all the time.

Proof of Life

I don't feel like going to work today
and my dutiful angel can't make me. Call in sick,
fake a cough like a C-lister, mumble something
on the message about feeling under the auspices.
Later, I walk over to Ron Sexsmith's house.
He answers the door wearing that shirt
with the little diamonds on it that he found
in a vintage shop in Helsinki. If we weren't
such good friends, I'd steal it off his back.
I tell Ron I woke up this morning wanting to listen
to the saddest song ever. Would he mind if
I had a look through his vast collection of sad songs?
Ron's game, so we settle in. I throw another 45
on the turntable and Ron says, "Sorry, not feeling it,"
tossing it onto an unruly pile on the floor. "Next!"
Ron says he once cried non-stop for a week,
cried so long and hard he ended up in hospital on an IV,
but that was back in the 80s. He's really quite happy now.
Ron says the selfie of him at Elton John's party
doesn't count as proof of life, though he likes
the one with Tom Waits at the butterfly conservatory.
Maybe he'll get it blown up and framed. Ron says
he had a dream about *Voyager*'s gold record: Ladies
and gentlemen, Blind Willie has left the solar system.
Ron relates a little-known fact about Gertrude Stein
and James Joyce's tailor, followed by an unpardonable pun.
The sun comes out and Ron draws thick velvet drapes
the colour of merlot so the mood remains undiluted.
"There's no time like the present to dwell on the past,"
muses Ron, as I dig in the crates on my knees.
Ron's cellphone rings and he lets it go to voicemail.

Ron says the whole world has gone straight to voicemail.
He confides he hates it when Elvis Costello calls him Ronnie.
Next time that git wants to go hat shopping, he can go alone.
Ron says the human heart is a transistor radio.
We keep listening. Together we'll find it, the saddest song
that ever was sung, and when we do, we'll wear it out.

The Early Bird

gets the overworked waitress who yearns
to be an occupational therapist and/or
win a singing competition. Her faux
familiarity as she focuses on a fly-speck
above my left shoulder: "Hi Luv, what'll it be?"
Speaking of birds, on the way here, I stopped
to peer at a scruffy curbside bush. What a din!
Its innermost branches were a teeming tenement.
It was as though the tree itself were singing.
What variety of shrub, which species of bird?
Beats me. In the interview, the over-latte-ed
VP probed, "What's your super power?" I might have
answered *grammar* or *an unassailable ennui* but,
having had my share of Rorschach tests, I said
the first thing that entered my head. *Poof!*
Right there in the boardroom, a thought bubble
emanated from an empty chair, rose on a micro-eddy
of coffee breath to the ceiling, burst without sound.
I don't expect a callback. God, it's deafening in here.
The *scrape-scrape-scrape* of knives and forks on plates,
the runny yolk of other tables' talk, the buttery
blah blah: I soak it up like white toast. My mother
taught me never to lie. There's nothing under my clothes
except more nothing. How scrupulously the waitress
avoids my eye. I'd really like another glass of water
and the cheque, please. I could sign my name
in the air all day long, nobody would come.

A Fine Place to Visit

All-Inclusive

Up the beach from the supper club's sprawling
patio where beleaguered servers thread the crowd
bearing trays of watered-down Cuba Libres
and grilled mahi-mahi on skewers, near the striped
changing huts and sea kayaks on steel racks,
two men pace figure eights in the sand, their faces
lit by cellphone screens. One sports a loud
shirt and a fresh sunburn, the other, darker
skinned, wears a once-white apron and hairnet.
They circle, pivoting on sandalled heels.
It's a wary dance, the boundaries invisible
yet understood. The elusive green
bars were here yesterday. You know
because you stood in this same spot yourself,
rumour of its whereabouts having spread like a cough
through the buffet line. There's always something
that can't wait: a friend's birthday, someone
in a nursing home, a child to wish goodnight
before the sitter switches out the light; niggles, logistics,
some little piece of news. The odd couple
commiserates silently—the one who chafes
at his leisure, the other on a smoke break.
What they have to say won't stay bottled up;
what they want to hear is the one thing
that will permit them sleep. But the satellites
won't cooperate: the night air carries
only the surf's white noise, merengue
from the resort casino on the next point.
It's an old story: figures on a far shore,
hands raised to the sky, searching for a signal.

Two tiny lights like fireflies engulfed by dark
inhuman scenery. The drone of scouring waves,
the moon stirring the iron filings of the sea.

It Has to Do with Velocity

Mass times acceleration. It's difficult to judge.
The tracks, anchored to the gravel

ballast bed with spikes, are matter-of-fact,
their symbolism right there on the surface

for all to see, but the train is illusory.
The engine's roar lags behind

the freight cars; the sound that precedes
the train as it speeds toward you

is uncannily quiet—10,000 tonnes of *hush*.
Now you see it, off in the distance, lazy

and picturesque, lumbering across the fields,
taking its sweet time. Watch it dissolve

in the haze, hunker behind a low hill,
reappear at its leisure. The by-and-by

lulls; noonday sun leaves you light-headed,
heated creosote like a jock's cologne.

Way over there, then right on top of you,
the slow emergency lollygagging into matter, shit

just got real. The train has nothing but time
and it wants to spend it all on you.

We: Outro

In the forests, we took a pecuniary interest,
reserved for them a hallowed place

in our memory. *Everything must go.*
We found loopholes in intractable vows,

went round and round
like unclaimed luggage on a carousel.

Plain speech became a pastoral:
the sound of one human voice

speaking to another replaced
by many voices talking at once.

Yea, though we drove though the valley
of the shadow, the airbrushed faces

on the billboards, they smiled upon us,
and we believed we could buy our way out.

It was difficult to distinguish between
the things we loved and said we loved.

A world of hurt, but we had brilliant toys
to distract us. We saw with belated clarity

that we were enrolled in a crash course,
and that everything was on the final exam.

It came as quite a shock. How gone?
Real gone. All our gift cards unredeemed.

Not for Lack of Trying

He didn't become a raving thing,
at least not for long and never
in public. Decorum prevented him
from a personal injury at track level.
Nor did he devolve into what
she had foreseen: a drunk
and a shut-in, the fridge barren
except for expired eggs and condiments.
There are zones of disengagement
even he could not reach.
                              If anything,
he grew more gregarious.
He wandered the city, brave
face painted on, lopsided grin.
He'd strike up conversations with strangers
on the subway, stop at bars in the afternoon
to nurse a beer and stare at the flat screen
closed-captioning the news: on the markets,
a day of losses; another woman's body
found in a suitcase; meteorologists
tracking a highly unusual storm.
My friends, to the bad old days
when the worst was yet to come.

The Itinerary

is poorly written or else it loses
something in translation: *On day two,*

*we journey into Germany, quaint wine
villages overlooking the Magnificent Rhine....*

Six countries in eight days by motorcoach,
Europe's greatest hits on a loop, somebody's

idea of leisure. You didn't want to go,
but your daughter insisted: "Dad, it's been over

two years ..." The Venice stop: quick trip
down the canal in the rain with a sullen gondolier,

guided tour of the glass-blowing factory, then a late
lunch at a bad *ristorante* with an uneventful wine list.

If the Blackshirts were still in vogue, the sommelier
would be stood against a wall. Were it not for Jocelyn

of Jocelyn's School of Dance, wasp-thin,
her long, long legs, corded muscle, orangey tan,

you couldn't bear it at all. It started in a Swiss hotel:
she grabbed you by the arm, waltzed you through

the lobby, much to the concierge's chagrin.
You were like George and Gracie,

terrorizing the bus driver with vaudeville
routines and pitchy opera tunes. In Florence, you

necked like thirtysomethings on the Ponte Vecchio.
On the *must-do Vatican walking tour*, your off-key

"Ave Maria" echoed in the apse of St. Peter's—
shushed by a Cardinal. It'll make the highlight reel.

"I loved my husband, but he's gone and I get
kind of lonesome," she said, Midwest direct.

Over a crackly line, you tell your daughter,
"She's your mother's exact opposite,

but she makes me laugh." How long has it been?
Day seven: Avignon. Tomorrow, Paris. Last stop.

Everything is arranged. Your daughter's already
given her a nickname: "the old dog's new trick."

If she accepts your terms, you'll fly home together
to meet the family. If not, you'll always have

Lucerne, *a beautiful small city in the heartland,
in and of itself, a fine place to visit.*

Fresco in the Rainy Season

A day in which anything might happen
and nothing does, of course. Yawn, scratch
the scab on your elbow. Let the mind
off its leash to ramble through memory's
fertile crescent. The beginning is persuasive,
tactile; the figures create their own
shallow depths. Your marriage, a sabbatical
in which you travelled from loneliness,
an all-too-brief interregnum between wars.
There were good years; others woefully
misspent, wearing the pattern off linoleum.
Did she really think you wouldn't notice
the bruises behind her knees? The rest
isn't worth repeating. When she left,
she took everything, the cat sedated
in the carrier, its pink tongue lolling.
What followed? A kind of blur, as you recall.
There were pills, whisky, winter's long
soliloquy to the tableware: *I knew her when
she was still in watercolours.* She should've stayed
put in the mural business. But it's much too easy
now to arrive at the foregone conclusion.
To get anywhere, you have to leave
the odd pair of dirty underwear behind,
a little something for the chambermaid.

The Epistemology of Balloons

The boy trudging with his mother
along the windy street is little,
and the bouquet of helium balloons
he's sea-anchored to is very large
and cumbersome. Fine motor skills
are a work in progress. So far, most things
have wanted to stay put or else
to crash down with a satisfying thud, but these
bright orange balloons have minds
of their own. They twist and tug at his grip
on their strings—any moment they might
lift him into the air. The thought
produces a muddle of pleasure and terror
he'll wait years to put a name to.
Anyone can guess what happens next, but
to the boy, it comes as a big surprise: "The sky
took my balloons!" Away they go, over the roofs
toward a blue gap between high-rises
and building cranes, which angle
like giant pinball paddles. If they don't
snag and go pop, they just might make it
all the way across the lake, coming down
in Buffalo or Rochester, but you wouldn't
wish that on anyone or anything, not even
a balloon. Were the mother to speak,
her words would come out strange. *Hold on
tight* is a rule of thumb, but sometimes
a lighter touch is required. The boy's
exaggerated gasp as good a response as any.
Once in a while (don't count on it),

what has been taken is returned
to us. "They're huge!" The snowflakes
that have just now begun lazily to fall.

Magnified Twenty Diameters

From "Studies among the Snow Crystals During the Winter of 1901–2, with Additional Data Collected During Previous Winters," by Mr. Wilson A. Bentley, dated Jericho, Vt., June 10, 1902

The question now naturally arises: Is there no limit
to the number of distinct forms, or may we assume
that, if our study be sufficiently prolonged,
there will come a time when new patterns
will rarely or never be found, the designs
merely reproductions or duplicates of those
already photographed? A partial answer
seems to be indicated by the number
of new patterns that were obtained from the past
winter's storms—greater than any
previous single winter. This fact,
coupled with the certainty that
the number of individual crystals that go to form
the snowfall of even one storm, is so vast
that one, or many observers, may never
hope to find and see anything more than
an absolutely insignificant fraction of
the whole, leads us to the conclusion
that, during all future time and so long as
there shall be observers to search for them,
new designs will continue to be found.

The Van

Doubtless it has carried drum kits, guitars, and Marshall stacks,
lumber from old barns, bushels of organic kale,
and transported poets, punks, and Rastafarians from one mattress
on the floor to another. The interior smells of patchouli,
beeswax, vegan spunk, and spilled beer. Surely someone
has quoted Chomsky, run fingers through a pixie cut,
placed a wildflower behind an elfin ear. A water-damaged copy
of David Foster Wallace's *Infinite Jest* props up a Coleman lantern.
Its spare tire is now a backyard swing off Roncesvalles.
Through Detroit in a blizzard, to Banff and over
the Vermilion Pass, as far south as old Mexico, and all night
across the Prairies to meet a girl. Seen rocking
on the playa at Burning Man and parked outside a yurt,
disassembled in a Customs garage at the Peace Arch
Border Crossing and put together again. (They found nothing.)
The engine, converted to run on grease-trap fat, starts up
with a Tom Waits purr. Its radiator has been pissed in.
It's gone 300,000 klicks; with any luck, good for another
hundred before it's abandoned in a municipal lot
or sold to a friend to fund a one-way ticket home.

The New Music

One minute you're a child, amazed
by the god-light leaking through clouds;
the next, dressed like an antiquarian
bookseller, creeping the Facebook page
of the one who got away, recently deceased.
When you think of all the times you said,
Just a sec, you want them all back.
You'd stow them with your passport
and your father's gold watch, recognition
for thirty years of service hand-tooling
replacement parts for obsolete machines.
One day, you know every song on the radio;
the next, all your favourite singers are dead.
You'd pour out your pickle jar of moments
like a boy counting his piggy-bank spoils,
letting them sieve through your fingers,
the cellar-must of sweat and copper.

The Nostalgist

Of archaisms, I am overly fond, it's true.
I check *The Facebook* to see if we're still on
for the *moving picture show*. And yes, I have
been known to obsess over what's written in
the dead wax. The past's last diehard evangelist,
I tap my toe to "Gimme a Pigfoot" by Bessie Smith
with Buck and His Band live at the Apollo, 1933,
on what I insist on calling the *gramophone*.
Walled in by records and books, it's as though
the house is made of them, as if they alone
prop up the ceiling. The blue bin *overfloweth*
with wine bottles and rinsed cat food tins.
The present's infatuation with minimalism
leaves me cold and bereft as a *bookshelf*
sans books, sans anything but one antique
inkwell adrift in a curated white space.
The brusque charmlessness of a condominium
lobby or the waiting room of an upscale
clinic where no one has to wait long.
This sanitized 1960s version of the future
makes me lonely for the *pshhhkkkkkkrrrr*
kakingkakingkaking tshchchchchchchchcch
⋆ding⋆ding⋆ding of the dialup modem, machines
awkwardly shaking hands over an analogue line.
May all our moments of connection be so
makeshift, so halting, so laborious.

The Photographer of Snowflakes

As a boy, he tried to sketch them,
but his pencil couldn't scurry fast enough
before the designs melted or sublimed in air.
He wanted to hold them in his mind
but they were already losing resolution.

Later, he would stand for hours
in the cold with a bellows camera
mated to a microscope, waiting
for the first snowflakes to commence
their twitchy, wind-tossed descent.

His subjects didn't like to pose;
with the feathers of a severed turkey wing,
he'd coax them gently, gently under the lens.
Conditions had to be just right: too warm
and their uniqueness would dissolve
before his eyes, too cold and they'd shatter.

Some winters, he'd capture only a handful.
Other years, they'd come all in a flurry.
His life's work, five thousand intimate portraits,
the glass plates rejected by the Smithsonian,
sold for five cents apiece. He died—I swear

I couldn't make this up—of pneumonia
after walking home six miles through a blizzard.
If you're going to die, why not in a storm
of devotion, after looking long and hard,
that the bits of pure beauty might be seen.

Even if it's a myth that there are
no two alike, I choose to believe it.
You have to believe in something.

Have you ever watched a dog
playing in fresh snow? It's of this
particular happiness I speak.
The sky gives it away for a song.

We: An Apologia

We loved the idea of trees and occasionally
to stroll among them. We loved how quiet
the city when it snowed and the view
from the air as we flew. Sleek and laminar,
we hurtled from one instant to the next.
We had been given a broad mandate: subdue
the continents, the sea and sky, fortify
the savage border. It was written.
We were the bee's knees, the mutt's nuts.
Our enlightenment was collateral.
We recalibrated the detectors.
We perfected the machine-human interface.
We left our footprints in the dust of other worlds.
We didn't know what we didn't
know. We disabled the fail-safes.
We reverse-engineered the Big Bang.
We reintroduced the wolves.
We *mea-culpa*-ed toward the door.
And we loved to dance.

The Horse You Rode in On

is very tired. Its sides heave
like the bellows of a great forge.
Steam pours from flared nostrils
as from a smokestack, pinkish
froth around its lips like scum
on the surface of a tailings pond.

What was it that couldn't wait?
A lover, a train, a satchel
of gold dust, a tarnished star
pinned to a vest pocket, a hanging tree?
What faint hope or festering grudge
did it bear across the miles, hooves
pounding salt pan like pistons?

Its coat has seen better days,
storm-scoured, thorn-scratched, spur-gouged.
Its mane is matted, its shedding tail
a tattered pennant, flanks caked
with trail dust and glistening salts.
Who or what pursued you
that you would travel so far so fast
without rest? A posse of ghosts?
Was it a voice on the wind or a vision
of the desperate near future
that led you relentlessly into the heat
shimmer of what's next?

It's a wonder your mount
didn't collapse beneath you,
fall on its knees, spilling out its last

few breaths like a tipped-over
brazier of burning coals.
But it carried you. Whatever
you thought was going to happen
is already over. The party
you were in such a hurry to meet
is sober past caring and in no mood
for excuses: *What kept you? You're late.*

Notes

The book's epigraph is from Graham Foust's poem "The Old Thing" from *Time Down to Mind* (Chicago: Flood Editions, 2015).

"Pastoral": The line "And who is sufficient for these things?" is from 2 Corinthians 2.16.

"The Upstarts" is for John Smith. This origin story owes a debt to biologists Lyn Margulis and Dorian Sagan, whose theory on the origin of complex cells, called symbiogenesis, focuses on cooperation as opposed to Darwinian selfishness; to Mark and Dianna McMenamin's book *Hypersea: Life on Land* (New York: Columbia UP, 1994); and to mineralogist Vladimir Vernadsky, who called living matter "animated water."

"Evolved from the Invisible," "Introduction to Unarmed Combat," and "Magnified Twenty Diameters" are found poems composed from the sources noted.

"An Arkansas Love Story" is in memory of Frank Stanford and C. D. Wright.

"Birds Fall Dead in Arkansas" incorporates found material from many sources into its aural collage including song lyrics, TV commercials, 9-1-1 calls, online news articles, and comments posted in response to them. The poem owes a particular debt to the following:

Choi, Charles. "Why are Birds Falling from the Sky?", *National Geographic News*, January 6, 2011.

CNN Wire Staff. "Massive fish kill blankets Arkansas River," *CNN.com*, January 3, 2011.

Dillow, Clay. "What Cataclysm Killed the Birds in Arkansas (and Louisiana, and Sweden)? Maybe None," *Popular Science*, January 6, 2011.

McLaughlin, Erin. "Dead Blackbirds Fall from the Sky Again in Beebe, Arkansas, on New Year's Eve," ABC *News* via *World News*, January 1, 2012.

Townsend, Catherine. "'So rough that our pit bull got stolen'," *MailOnline* via *DailyMail*, February 20, 2013.

The epigraph is from Ovid, *Metamorphoses*, Book XI. Trans. by Mary M. Innes. London: Penguin Books, 1955.

"Stars Fell on Alabama" is the title of a 1934 jazz standard composed by Frank Perkins with lyrics by Mitchell Parish. It refers to a Leonid meteor shower observed in 1833.

The poem quotes Delta Blues legend CeDell Davis's original song "If You Like Fat Women" from his album *Feel like Doin' Something Wrong*, Fat Possum Records, 1994.

Rest in peace, Mindy McCready, 1975–2013.

"Uncanny Valley": The line "Nothing is quote / unquote real anymore" is taken from the blog post "The Future of CGI Is Using Motion Capture to Recreate Inanimate Objects" by Casey Chan, *Gizmodo.com*, January 22, 2012.

"For the Beauty of Winona Ryder": The Lawrence Ferlinghetti poem referred to is "Retired Ballerinas, Central Park West" from *These Are My Rivers: New and Selected Poems, 1955–1993* (New York: New Directions, 1993).

"The Path of the Hero" is in memory of Darrell Gray.

"We Like You for This" includes several questions found in The Global Health Center's General Health Questionnaire: http://www.globalhealingcenter .com/general-health-questionnaire.html.

"Wilderness of Signs" is after Kevin Connolly's poem "Drift" from his collection *Drift* (Toronto: Anansi, 2005) and borrows its title from that poem's last line.

"Proof of Life" is for Ron Sexsmith (who, in truth, I've never met, though his songs are old friends).

"The Epistemology of Balloons" is after Wilde Collins who, at the time of writing, was age two and a half.

"The Photographer of Snowflakes" is based on the life of Wilson A. "Snowflake" Bentley (1865–1931), a pioneer in photomicrography who became the world's leading authority on snowflakes. The phrase "bits of pure beauty" is his.

Acknowledgements

Some of these poems first appeared in *Arc Poetry Magazine, Canadian Notes and Queries, Cordite Poetry Review* (Australia), *Dusie, The Fiddlehead, Grain, Humanist Perspectives, Lemon Hound, The Malahat Review, newpoetry.ca*, and *Poetry Daily*. My thanks to the editors of these publications.

"All-Inclusive," which originally appeared on *Lemon Hound*, was selected by editors Helen Humphreys, Molly Peacock, and Anita Lahey for inclusion in the anthology *Best Canadian Poetry in English 2016* (Tightrope, 2016).

"Pastoral" was an "Editor's Choice" in the 2014 *Arc Poetry Magazine* Poem of the Year contest. "The Van" and "Self-Portrait as Archaic Torso" were long-listed for the 2014 CBC Poetry Prize. An earlier incarnation of "We Like You for This" received third place in *Grain Magazine*'s 2016 Short Grain Poetry Contest.

"I Want to Love More" appears in *Translating Horses: The Line, The Thread, The Underside* edited by Jessica Hiemstra and Gillian Sze (London: Baseline Press, 2015).

Special thanks to Julie and Ian Dennison, Janet McOrmond, Steve Noyes, John Reibetanz, John Smith, Matthew Tierney, and Andy Weaver for their generosity and perspicuity in reading and commenting on early drafts of many of these poems.

Thanks to all who lent their ears: John Barton, Catherine Greenwood, David Hickey, Jessica Hiemstra, Adrienne Barrett Hofman, Robert and

Margaret Hoops, Karen Schindler, David Seymour, Charmaine Tierney, and Jan Zwicky.

Many thanks to my editor Helen Guri for pushing these poems, gently but firmly, out of their comfort zone.

The Canada Council for the Arts, the Ontario Arts Council, and the Toronto Arts Council provided financial support during the completion of this book.

Steve McOrmond is the author of three previous collections of poetry, most recently *The Good News about Armageddon* (Brick Books, 2010). His second collection, *Primer on the Hereafter* (Wolsak and Wynn, 2006), was awarded the Atlantic Poetry Prize. His debut collection, *Lean Days* (Wolsak and Wynn, 2004), was shortlisted for the Gerald Lampert Award. Originally from Prince Edward Island, he lives in Toronto.